Books by Barbara Cohen

The Carp in the Bathtub
Thank You, Jackie Robinson
Where's Florrie?
Bitter Herbs and Honey
Benny
R My Name Is Rosie
The Binding of Isaac

THE BINDING OF
ISAAC

BARBARA COHEN
ILLUSTRATED BY
CHARLES MIKOLAYCAK

LOTHROP, LEE & SHEPARD COMPANY
A Division of William Morrow & Co., Inc.
New York

To Leah
who had the idea first.

THE GRANDFATHER WAS OLD AND blind. His grandchildren, who sat on his lap and at his feet, listened to him tell what happened when he was a boy.

"When I was two, I no longer nursed at my mother's breast," said the grandfather, whose name was Isaac. "And so my father Abraham made a great feast in honor of my weaning. He invited the chief men of the country to come, and their wives and children, and all their servants. Five hundred people came and they feasted for three days and three nights in my honor. And when they left, they all took with them gifts of wine and olive oil."

"Our father Jacob never made such a feast for me," said Reuben, who was the eldest.

"Oh, well," replied his grandfather, "my father and mother had waited such a long time for me. My father had only two children, Ishmael and me. My father loved Ishmael, but Ishmael hated me."

"Why did he hate you, Grandfather?" asked Judah, who was already as tall and as handsome as a prince.

"Abraham loved our grandfather Isaac best," explained Joseph, who was dressed in a glorious many-colored coat his father Jacob had given him. "Isn't that so, Grandfather?"

"Just so," said the grandfather, and he nodded. "My father loved me better than Ishmael and for that Ishmael hated me. My mother, Sarah, was my father's true wife, and Ishmael's mother, Hagar, was a servant. Ishmael feared that when our father died, all that he had would come to me. At the weaning feast there were games, and Ishmael shot at targets with his bow and arrow. Sometimes his shot went wild, as if by accident. But Ishmael was a skillful archer. My mother thought his wild shots were not accidents, and she was afraid that one of the arrows would find its way to me. So she asked my father to send Ishmael and his mother away."

"Did he do that?" asked Naphtali, who was also a servant's son. Isaac's grandchildren had the same father, but they had been born of four different mothers. "Did he send his own child away?" Naphtali asked again.

"Yes, he did," said the grandfather. "God told my father He had other plans for Ishmael. My father Abraham sent Ishmael away, although he loved him. For he loved me more. He loved me more than he loved the sun or the moon or the stars."

"He loved you more than he loved any-thing," said Asher, the plump, generous one.

"No," said the grandfather. "He didn't love me more than anything. But God was afraid he did. God waited, and then one day when I was no longer a baby, God called to my father: 'Abraham.'"

"My father answered, 'Here I am.'

"'Take your son,' God said.

"'But I have two sons,' my father said.

"'Your only son,' God replied.

"'But each is the only one of his mother,' my father said.

"'Whom you love,' God replied.

"'But I love both,' my father said.

"'Even Isaac,'" God replied. "Take your son, your only son, whom you love, even Isaac, and go to the land of Moriah, and sacrifice him there to me on the top of the mountain.'"

"But your father wouldn't do that," said Levi. "Not even for God."

"Be quiet and listen," said the grandfather. "Listen to what happened. The next morning my father got up very early. He woke me and told me we were going on a journey. He took two servants with him and a donkey to carry the wood that he had chopped. We traveled through the wilderness for three days. For three days we traveled, and I didn't know where we were going, and I didn't know why."

"Didn't you ask?" Zebulun, who was always curious, wanted to know.

"I asked," the grandfather replied, "and my father told me we were going to make a sacrifice to God. I thought it strange to go so far to make a sacrifice, but my father said God had picked out the place for the sacrifice Himself. I knew that my father talked to God, and that there was no arguing with either of them.

"We came to the bottom of a high mountain, and my father said to his servants, 'Stay here with the donkey. The boy and I will go up to the top of the mountain. There we'll worship God, and then we'll come back to you.'

"My father took the wood we had brought with us from home, and he gave it to me to carry. In one hand he had a pot of coals from our hearth so that he could kindle a fire on the mountain. In the other hand, he carried a knife. We began to climb the mountain, both of us together."

"It seemed strange to me—wood, fire, knife, but no calf or lamb or kid to offer to God. So I said, 'My father.'

"And he answered me, 'Here I am, my son.'

"And I said, 'Here's the fire, and here's the wood, but where's the lamb to offer to God?'

"My father answered me, 'God will provide the lamb for the offering, my son.'

"So we climbed and climbed, both of us together. When we got to the top of the mountain, my father placed some large stones on top of piles of smaller stones to make an altar. He took the wood that I had carried and laid a fire in the altar. Still there was no sign of a calf or a lamb or a kid, and I said to my father once again, 'Where's the lamb to offer to God?'

"Then my father said, 'You are the lamb, my son.' And he laid me down on the altar, and he took rope and tied me there so that I couldn't move."

"Didn't you cry? Didn't you scream? Didn't you struggle?" urged Gad, who was a fighter.

"There was such sadness in my father's eyes," the grandfather went on in a dreamy voice as if he hadn't even heard the question. "He moved so slowly, so heavily. I didn't make a sound. I didn't make a move. I couldn't."

The grandfather paused for a moment, and his strong old arm tightened around Benjamin, who was the baby and sat on his lap.

For a little while, none of the children spoke. Then Simeon said, "My father would never do that to me. Even if God did ask him to."

"Well, God didn't ask your father to," the

grandfather replied sharply. "He's asked it of no one else since."

"Don't be angry with me, Grandfather," said Simeon.

"I'm not angry, Simeon," said the grandfather in a gentler voice. "I know how you feel. I couldn't believe my father would do it to me either. And if he could, then what was the use of living? And that's why I lay there so quiet and so still. I didn't believe it was happening. Even when my father took the knife in his hand, and stretched forth his arm, and the tip of the knife touched my chest, I didn't believe it."

"What happened then, Grandfather?" asked Dan, the logical one. "You're here today to tell us the story, so you didn't die."

"Something died," the grandfather replied. "I didn't die; only something in me died. Then a voice called out from heaven. 'Abraham, Abraham,' the voice called. It was God's voice.

"'Here I am,' my father replied.

"'Don't touch the boy,' the voice said. 'Don't touch him with the knife or with your hand. I know now you love Me more than anything, because you were willing to give Me your son, your only son.'

"Then my father stood up. In the bushes he saw a ram, caught by the horns. My father untied me, and we took the ram and bound it to the altar. With his knife, my father killed the ram, and then we lit the fire and made an offering of the ram to God.

"The voice of God spoke to my father again. This time God said, 'Because you have done this thing, because you have been willing to give Me your son, your only son, you will be blessed. You will have as many great-great-great-great grandchildren as there are stars in the sky and grains of sand upon the shore. Because you listened to Me, your great-great-great-great grandchildren shall rule whole cities and bring blessings to all the people of the earth.'"

"And will all that happen?" asked Judah, the prince.

"Yes," replied their grandfather Isaac. "All that will happen—if not to you, then to those who come after you. And none of you will ever be asked to sacrifice your children. God will not ask anyone to do that again. That's the promise he made to my father, Abraham, and to me."

"But Grandfather," said Dinah, who was the only girl, "if the voice of God had not come out of heaven and told your father not to sacrifice you, do you think he would have? Do you think your father would have killed you?"

"I don't know," replied the grandfather. "And since I didn't know, that question stood between me and my father as long as he lived. On the way home, he told me how God had commanded him to sacrifice me, but I never asked him if he really would have done it, and he never told me."

"We do what we must do," said Issachar, who worked hard in the fields. "Our great-grandfather Abraham had sworn to serve God in every way. He had to do what God told him to do."

"I don't think he would have done it,"

Dinah insisted. "What would he have said to Sarah when he came back if our grandfather Isaac had not been with him? And God didn't think he'd do it either. And God didn't want to find out, for sure."

The grandfather smiled. "God must have known, Dinah. But I never knew, and even my father couldn't be sure. But God—God knows. And my father and I—we had to be content with not knowing. My father and I, and all of you—in the end what we do is what God wills us to do."

"The important thing, Grandfather," said Joseph, the dreamer who dreamed the truth, "is that you didn't die. You didn't die. You lived. You are here."

"That's right, Joseph," his grandfather said to him. "That's the important thing."

BARBARA COHEN, perhaps best known for that little classic *The Carp in the Bathtub,* is also highly regarded for her novels, which include *Thank You, Jackie Robinson, Benny,* and *Bitter Herbs and Honey.* Mrs. Cohen, a newspaper columnist and former English teacher as well as novelist, grew up in New Jersey in an inn operated by her widowed mother. Today, with her husband Gene and their three daughters, she still lives in the same vicinity.

CHARLES MIKOLAYCAK, a distinguished graphics designer and illustrator, has received many honors for his children's books, some of which have been ALA Notables and Children's Book Council Showcase selections. He and his wife Carole, a magazine picture editor, live in New York City.